TURKISH PEARS IN AUGUST

TURKISH PEARS IN AUGUST

TWENTY-FOUR RAMAGES
BY ROBERT BLY

EASTERN WASHINGTON UNIVERSITY PRESS

12   11   10   09   08   07   5   4   3   2   1   Printed in Canada.

Turkish Pears in August was first published in 2005 by Midnight Paper Sales in a letterpress edition of 150 copies. The present edition incorporates four poems and two illustrations that did not appear in the original edition.

Cover design by A. E. Grey

Library of Congress Cataloguing-in-Publication Data

Bly, Robert.
Turkish pears in August : twenty-four ramages / by Robert Bly.
    p.   cm.
   "First published in 2005 by Midnight Paper Sales in a letterpress edition of 150 copies. The present edition incorporates four poems and two illustrations that did not appear in the original edition"—T.p. verso.
   ISBN-13: 978-1-59766-023-5 (alk. paper)
   I. Title.
   PS3552.L9T87 2007
   811'.54—dc22
                                         2007028001

Eastern Washington University Press | *Spokane and Cheney, Washington*

A NOTE ON THESE POEMS

A few years ago, I began to hear inside the stanza individual sounds such as *in* or *air* or *ar* call to each other. An *er* is a sort of being that cries out. What could we call a union of a consonant and a vowel? The word syllable is a ridiculous name for it; it's too Latinate and mute. These particles have more energy than the word "syllable" suggests. ⁊ Hearing these cries put me into a new country of poetry. I was not hiking among ideas or images or stories, but among tiny, forceful sounds. What would happen if I adopted *in* or *ar* as the center of a poem? Decisions on content would then depend on that. I let that happen. For length, I settled on eight lines, which is larger than a couplet but smaller than a sonnet. ⊄ Every poem, of course, has to have images and ideas and some sort of troubled speaker. But I began more and more to shift attention to the little mouths that cry out their own name. ⊄ I eventually accepted *ramage* as a title for this brief poem. The word occasionally appears as the name of a movement during some French compositions for flute; it is related to the French noun for "branch." We can hear the root of that in "ramify." ⊄ The tunings of these things is like tuning on horseback some sort of stringed instrument from the Urals. Each time you try to add one more of the chosen sound particles, new nouns abruptly enter the poem, and one has to deal with them.

He was seeing all the fibres of natural history around him.

NIGHT IN THE GARDEN

Dust made somnolent by pine branches holds
Up the dark-headed, dangerous psalm-singer.
He cures the sick, raises Lazarus from the grave,
Insists that only John shall be exalted.
Demons scatter salt on the stony ground.
These pains and wrongs have been here a long time.
He clears the stains from Thomas's coat, makes
Arrangements for a donkey in Jerusalem.

WOMEN AND MEN

We'd like to know what women want-some want
Heaven and earth joined. Some men want sawn
Boards, roads diverging, and jackdaws flying,
Heaven and earth parted. Women love to see
Strangers fed, children fed and laughing,
Daughters in seats of honor, canvases with Venus
And a naked man, doves returning at dusk,
Cloths folded, and giants sitting down at table.

KRISHNAMURTI AND HIS STUDENTS

The young men reading Krishnamurti say no
To womanly joy, orioles, wagtails, mud,
Rancid songs, the hair of drowning persons,
Bare ankles, the brandy-breath lost in cold,
All the glee bandits feel by the ocean.
That's all right, but it's not the whole story.
Krishnamurti himself loved orioles and wagtails,
As well as handsome women and flooded fields.

THE OLD STONE ON THE MOUNTAIN

Grief lies close to the roots of laughter.
Both love the cabin open to the traveler,
The ocean apple wrapped in its own leaves.
How can I be close to you if I'm not sad?
The animal pads where no one walks.
There is a gladness in the not-caring
Of the bear's cabin; and in the gravity
That makes the stone laugh down the mountain.

TURKISH PEARS

Sometimes a poem has her own husband
And children, her nooks and gardens and kitchens,
Her stairs, and those sweet-armed serving boys
Who carry veal in shiny copper pans.
Some poems do give plebeian sweets
Tastier than the chocolates French diners
Eat at evening, and old pleasures abundant
As Turkish pears in the garden in August.

SO MUCH TIME

December's foolishness, embers fall, tempters
Fly up into the dreamt palace. Things move
Slowly in the soul. By that slowness we guess
We've already been grieving a hundred years.
Old men and women know how much time
Can go by while praying. The soul flows
At its own slow pace. There is so much time,
We can stay in grieving another hundred years.

ORION THE GREAT WALKER

Orion, that old hunter, floats among the stars
Firmly... the farms beneath his feet. How long
It takes for me to walk in grief like him.
Seventy years old, and still placing my feet
So hopefully each night on the ground.
How long it takes for me to agree to sorrow.
But that great walker follows his dogs,
Hunting all night among the disappearing stars.

FOR THE OLD GNOSTICS

The Fathers put their trust in the end of the world
And they were wrong. The Gnostics were right and not
Right. Dragons copulate with their knobby tails.
Some somnolent wealth rises unconcerned,
Yes, over there! Ponderous stubborn
Sorrow weighs down the flying Gospels.
The dragons copulate with their knobby tails.
The untempered soul grumbles in empty light.

THE WATCHER OF VOWELS

How lovely it is to write with all these vowels:
Body, Thomas, the codfish's psalm. The gaiety
Of form comes from the labor of its playfulness.
We are drunkards who never take a drop.
We all become ditch-diggers like Brahms.
No, no, we are like that astronomer
Who watches the great sober star return
Each night to its old place in the night sky.

THE HERMIT AT DAWN

Early in the morning the hermit wakes, hearing
The roots of the fir tree stir beneath his floor.
Someone is there. That strength buried
In earth carries up the summer world. When
A man loves a woman, he nourishes her.
Dancers strew the lawn with the light of their feet.
When a woman loves the earth, she nourishes it.
Earth nourishes what no one can see.

WHAT IS SORROW FOR?

What is sorrow for? It is a storehouse
Where we store wheat, barley, corn and tears.
We step to the door on a round stone,
And the storehouse feeds all the birds of sorrow.
And I say to mself: Will you have
Sorrow at last? Go on, be cheerful in autumn,
Be stoic, yes, be tranquil, calm;
Or in the valley of sorrows spread your wings.

A RAMAGE FOR THE MOUNTAIN

Silent in the moonlight, no beginning or end.
So the binding things are lost, then found again,
The tines dug out of snow, the singing so low
The other cannot hear it. Some sounds do fit
Thick cords and strong fingers. Slowly the mountain
Enters the man who walks on its slopes alone.
He walks, he sits down, he finds a stone;
No one has seen it, he sits down and is alone.

SILENT IN THE MOONLIGHT

Silent in the moonlight, no beginning or end.
Alone, and not alone. A man and woman lie
On open ground, under an antelope robe.
They sleep under animal skin, looking up
At the old, clear stars. How many years?
The robe thrown over them, rough,
Where they sleep. Outside, the moon, the plains
Silent in the moonlight, no beginning or end.

THE PHEASANT CHICKS

"As soon as the master is untied, the bird soars."
That is what Tao Yuan Ming said one day.
"In the sad heat of noon the pheasant chicks
Spread their new wings in the moon dust."
Such glory, such persistence, such foolishness!
Does it matter whether we are sad or happy?
Our laughter goes back to the roots of trees.
An old sadness returns in the sorrowing dust.

LOVERS IN THE RIVER

Peony blossoms open in starlight. The lovers
Cross the river carefully, secretly, secretly.
All night horses stamp on the sandy island.
Husbands feel uneasy tonight. Their wives
Have gathered with Krishna in the river,
Their bodies sweetened by glad bones.
While David sings, stars fall into the sea; Uriah
Dies. . . It is the madness of the dark-faced God.

THE BIG-NOSTRILLED MOOSE

Horses go on eating the Apostle Island ferns.
Also sheep and goats; also the big-nostrilled moose
Who knocks down the common bushes
In his longing for earthly pleasure.
The moose's great cock floats in the lily pads.
That image calms us. His nose calms us.
Slowly, obstinately, we retrieve the pleasures
The Fathers, angry with the Gnostics, threw away.

THE GRACKLES

Grackles stroll about on the black floor of sorrow.
Rabbis robed in saffron feed them
Minnow bread... They come to meet you.
Moses and his black wife walk like birds
And dance. Among the stalks of wild timothy grass
The saddled horses drink from sorrow tanks.
But the grackles' toes are springy—they walk
Over the footprints the dreamer made last night.

THE BEAR'S CABIN

So in the bear's cabin I come to earth.
There are limits. Among all the limits
We know so few things. How is it I know
Only one river—its turns—and one woman?
The love of woman is the knowing of grief.
There are no limits to grief. The loving man
Simmers his porcupine stew. Among the tim-
Ber growing on earth grief finds roots.

THE MOTHER TURTLE

Climbing on shore to give her brood a home,
She gathers each day bits of primitive hay.
Being open to the phases of the moon,
She piles her leathery eggs at pale midnight.
Moving slowly in the night, she leaves her eggs
On the beach, covers them with gleaming sand.
Hundreds of gulls fly in, but a few of the young
Find their way to the enormous sea.

ABOUT HENRY DAVID THOREAU

Henry Thoreau abandoned his old scandalous life
To live among the sand cranes and the ants.
He wasn't a big back-thumper, but he
Kept company with his handsome language.
He couldn't be called a gallant lover, but he was firm.
He kept a lover's book telling which flower
Was likely to blossom today. Friends,
Beyond that, he lived extravagantly alone.

HEARD WHISPERS

The spider sways in October winds; she hears the whisk
Of the bat's foot as it leaves the branch, the groan
The bear makes far out on the Labrador ice,
The cry of the wren as the hurricane takes
The house, the cones falling, the sigh of the nun
As she dies, the whisper Jesus makes to
The woman drawing water, the nearly silent weeping
Of bones eager to be laid away in the grave.

TRISTAN AND ISOLDE

The glad body sings its four-legged tunes.
It has its honesty. Lovers know the obstinacy
Of the body, the grunts that say to spirit,
Gone, gone! The awl pulls from the leather;
The thread pulls from the needle's eye. Later
He seems good to her eyes, like a waterhole
Muddied by animals. Tristan and Isolde
Love their bawdy lodge, no north, no south.

THE SLIM FIR-SEEDS

The nimble oven bird, the dignity of pears,
The simplicity of oars, the imperishable
Engines inside slim fir-seeds, all of these
Hint how much we long for the impermanent
To be permanent. We want the hermit wren
To keep her eggs even during the storm;
We want eternal oceans. But we are perishable;
Friends, we are salty, impermanent kingdoms.

WANTING SUMPTUOUS HEAVENS

No one grumbles among the oyster clans,
And lobsters play their bone guitars all summer.
Only we, with our opposable thumbs, want
Heaven to be, and God to come, again.
There is no end to our grumbling; we want
Comfortable earth *and* sumptuous heaven.
But the heron standing on one leg in the bog
Drinks his rum all day, and is content.

Turkish Pears in August originally appeared in a letterpress edition of 150 copies, printed by Gaylord Schanilec at Midnight Paper Sales, with a cover of paper handcrafted by Bridget O'Malley. The poems are set in 14/18 Italian Old Style, and the illustrations are original wood engravings by Gaylord Schanilec. Both the Italian Old Style type and the Monument titling used on the title page were cast by Scott King for the letterpress edition. Four of the poems and two of the illustrations are new to this edition, which is otherwise a facsimile of the original.